Prison Segmentation For Mental Peace

Reverend Mike Wanner

Copyright

October 11, 2017

Reverend Mike Wanner

Selected Images Used by License

Table Of Contents

Table Of Contents 3
Introduction 4
1 - I am Writing This Book Because 5
2 - Book In Not To Be Used In Place of Professional Services 7
3 - The Intensity of Density 8
4 - Mental Concerns & Stress Can Increase Danger 9
5 - Power In Each Person 10
6 - Are The Best Resources Available? 11
7 - Vulnerable Prisoners 12
8 - Yoga Awareness 13
9 - The Effect Of Stigma 14
10 - Little Things - Big Difference 15
11 - One Idea Of Possibility 16
12 - Prisoners Could Be Triaged 18
13 - The Challenge Is To Make It Work 19
14 - Segmentation Could Influence A Lot 21
15 - Declaration Of Program Start 22
16 - Start Up Questions For Prisoners 23
17 - Time Block Design 24
18 - Opportunities Can Change A Lot 25
19 - Segmentation Could Change Surroundings 26
20 - Segmentation Could Take Many Forms 27
21 - Thank You 28
22 - Don't Worry Ever 29
23 - Resource Books 30
24 - Angels Please Prayers 32
25 - Private Channeling 33
26 - Reverend Mike Wanner 34

Introduction

Sources report that in America alone there are more than 2.3 million people in prison or jail and a significant portion of them may have mental health challenges.

There are many jurisdictions that place prisoners with mental health issues in prison instead of the health care system. There do not seem to be enough resources to handle all the medical health needs of all the prisoners.

The jurisdictions at the federal, state and more local levels have their budgets to manage, and the task is ongoing.

The topic of segmentation that I introduced in my last book can also be helpful in providing space which may just have a healthy, peaceful dynamic that while not remedial to mental health, it may help to avoid further agitation to those that are insufficient in personal peacefulness.

Treatment of those with mental health issues is a career and the people who work in that profession have skills that are awesome. Professional standards of care are costly to maintain, and the insurance coverage under most insurance plan seems to be very basic.

In my ambulance work over a quarter of a century, I have taken a number of people for mental health care, and caution is needed to prevent episodes that are not beneficial. I cannot even imagine the difficulty that correctional officers endure when they do not yet have a diagnosed condition.

1 - I am Writing This Book Because

In 2013, Angel Raphael invited me to visit a prison energetically. While delayed by other books, The invitation was honored in 2016, and that led to publishing the following books related to prisons:

1. *Angel Raphael Speaks Volume 4: Angels, Addicts, Alcoholics & Prisoners - Oh Yeah!*
2. *Angel Raphael Speaks Volume 5: Prisoners Caring for Alcoholics - Australia In Miniature   Projects Intro*
3. *Angel Raphael Speaks Volume 6: Prisoners Caring for Addicts - Australia In Miniature For   Addicts*
4. *Prison Jobs Now: Providing Care For Addicts And Alcoholics*
5. *Angel Raphael Speaks - Prisons (A Kindle only book -2013)*
6. *Contained Care Communities: Concept*
7. *Australia In Miniature*
8. *Prison Possibilities Dialogue Series: Concept*
9. *Prison Possibilities Dialogue Series: Volume 2 Dialogues*
10. *Prison Possibilities Dialogue Series: Volume 3 Dialogues*
11. *Prison Possibilities Dialogue Series: Volume 4 Dialogues*
12. *Prison Possibilities Dialogue Series: Volume 5 Dialogues*
13. *Prison Possibilities Voluntary Exile: Concept*
14. *Prison Possibilities Correction Coaches: Concept*
15. *Prison Possibilities for Mexicans: Is A Boat Better than A Wall?*
16. *Prison Possibilities Family Time: A Reason to Thrive!*
17. *Prison Genius Pool: "So Much Genius In Jail."*
18. *Prison Possibilities Access Systems: Prisoner Access by Request*
19. *Prisoner's Lawyers Can Save The American Economy: Make A Buck Doing It & Be Thanked!*
20. *Prisoner Family Talks, Days, Stays & Vacations: Connecting Helps Healing*
21. *Prisoner Writing Projects: Write To Heal, Start Over & Reconnect*
22. *Prison Cell Clearing & Blessing: Clear Entities, Chase Ghosts, and & Create Sacred Space*
23. *Prisoner Professors: Show You Are Aware Create Change With Care*

24. *Prison Reiki? Maybe Someday? A Gateway To Help Heal Prisons & America?*
25. *Judges and An Angel Rule On Possibilities: We Can Cut Sentences & Prison Costs*
26. *Ideas For Prison Wardens: Leadership Is Not Easy*
27. *Solitary Community: Could Community Support Cut Costs and Issues?*
28. *Prisoner Projects Communication Teams: Communications Can Change Lives*
29. *Motivating & Empowering Prisoners? Invite Prisoners To Find Their Motivation & Their Future*
30. *Prison Segmentation for Safety*
31. *Prison Segmentation for Security*
32. *Dowsing For Prisoners*
33. *Ex-Prisoners Possibilities with Real Estate Investors*

This book continues to carry the potential for rethinking that can help to reduce incarceration to those who we need to have there.

I want to trigger mindset shifts in the prisoners as well as employees and the community. We need a lot more Objective Productive Dialogues about Enhancing the lives of Prison Employees, Prisoners, Taxpayers and the Families of all.

2 - Book Is Not To Be Used In Place of Professional Services

This
Book
Is
Not
To
Be
Used
In
Place
of
Professional
Services

But Might Be Helpful To Reduce Risks

The Intensity Of Density Can Cause Enormous Stress

4 - Mental Concerns & Stress Can Increase Danger

I invite prison staff to be more aware of the intensity of density and how overcrowding can produce stress that could contribute to negative influences on them.

Remember that "What goes around comes around." (Anon.) Those with mental issues can be agitated in many ways.

A natural reaction for coping in times of stress is described as the Fight or Flight response. In prison, however, the flight is not possible.

A prisoner who is triggered may have nowhere to go and may feel the situation has no option. It may seem more like fight or fight.

The problem with no options is an intensification and perhaps consequences that could not be foreseen. Reactiveness can cause people to be hurt in the process, and sometimes there could be more trouble that could result in an extension of the sentence of a prisoner who overacts and hurts others.

Prison staff has a lot to do, and prisoners with mental crises can present many challenges because employees may not be trained or equipped with the resources they might need. I hope that staff can find resources that can ease any mental stress that might trigger prisoner reactiveness.

Resources that ease mental stress could be a safety valve that can help prisoners, staff, and taxpayers.

5 - Power In Each Person

Have you noticed that even in families, each person has their own unique personality? Individuality can be lost in prison, and the pattern of loss can keep repeating because it is familiar and established to a level like a default setting on a computer.

I have been writing about prison segmentation for safety and security, and I am hopeful that It can allow many prisoners to find a new level of personal peace. Of course, I am aware that there are more than six thousand individual incarceration facilities in America alone and the rules vary.

A peaceful, free person can think for themselves and be proactive in controlling stress and staying tranquil. Prisoners are not able to regulate their circumstances.

Prison staff has the need to deal with the reactiveness to the complications that mental health issues with stress provide.

I wish that I had all the answers to all the problems and I could lay them out for all the readers. It seems that I often say that the prison situation is complicated and that is true.

If many people feel powerless, that can trigger trouble, and it can add additional complexity. I would encourage all readers to act deliberately from a favorable view and help prisoners to not to lash out.

Staff personnel did not write the plans under which a facility works, but reasonableness may help everybody to keep trying. Positive Efforts are much more beneficial than anything else.

6 - Are The Best Resources Available?

While it is required by rules or law that prisoners receive adequate care, facility crowding may make the delivery of the care an enormous challenge. Every facility has definite plusses and difficulties, and prisoner care needs may be secondary to the primary job assigned to each facility which is incarceration.

The intensity of the density of prison creates stress for all, and that is why I am writing about the possibility of segmentation. The logic to the utilization of space around the clock is so there are fewer people in all areas at all times by using space to the optimal utility capacity over as many hours as feasible.

Fewer people in a confined space can lead to less dense energy interaction between the bodies of the people there. Decreasing density can promote personal peacefulness and a feeling of safety that might allow for a lessening of stress.

Peacefulness can set the stage for personal reflection and spiritual awakening which can have many benefits. Imagine the personal peace that can happen with the ability to hear oneself think.

Segmentation can be a fertile field of peace that can grow a crop of peaceful possibility. Add to that a predictable set of circumstances that are agreed on and a problem can be changed to an opportunity.

Performance essentials for success would not need to be complicated, but they would need to be measured and entirely predictable.

7 - Vulnerable Prisoners

Prisoners with mental illness are likely more vulnerable to stress reactivity than the general population. Segmentation may be able to help some prisoners to find some peace first so they can get some help later.

Prisons are typically overcrowded, and the intensity of human emotions could be detrimental to the most vulnerable in the crowd.

Stressed individuals do not always realize why they are stressed but the intensity of stress is prevalent throughout the country, and it is a frequent topic of business conversation.

I have a whole website devoted to stress, and you can visit it at http://www.StressReleaseCoach.com . That material and more is included in a book that I wrote called *Stress Release Energy Work: How To Cope* which is available on Amazon and Kindle

Ratcheting down the intensity of prison through segmentation could go a long way to help mitigate stress induced crises.

While Segmentation can help stabilize the living space for all residents, caution should be used to avoid declaring any health benefits to individuals who have issues.

It can be simple enough to talk about the peace that can flow from spaciousness while mentioning the advantages of segmentation for the freer settling of emotional charges.

8 - Yoga Awareness

There are a number of websites, books, and articles covering the benefits of Yoga for healing and mindfulness. I invite you to google Yoga In Prisons and see all the articles and book references that come up.

While Yoga is not a mental health technique per se, it can contribute significantly to a person's sense of tranquility which may help vulnerable people to stay away from a critical level of intensity. A Yoga program designed by a mental health professional can have an even more significant impact than a standard application.

There is a Prison Yoga Project which strives to provide men, women, and youth prisoners with a yoga and mindfulness practice as skills to use even when they're not doing yoga.

Their website is https://prisonyoga.org where you can get more information. Prison officials would be wise to invite their Mental Health Practitioner team to investigate the appropriateness of yoga for their facilities and their prisoners.

If the healthcare professional can approve the practices, the prisons may be able to calm their facilities, record caregiving to their residents and improve the quality of life for prison staff all at the same time.

Sacramento has a Yoga effort called The Yoga Seed Collective. Their website is http://www.theyogaseed.org/prisonyoga/

9 - The Effect Of Stigma

Mental Health has long carried a stigma which is not deserved. Mental Illness is a disease which is best cared for expediently like other illnesses.

Folks in need of mental health treatment can delay care because they are concerned about being labeled negatively. This delay can act as a barrier to a remedial course of treatment.

The National Alliance on Mental Illness, nicknamed NAMI, has a whole program to combat Stigma and promote effective treatment.

The goal of their program is Stigma-Free Care Receivers. Find out how you can take the pledge and help their efforts at https://www.nami.org/stigmafree

How You can help:

[Take The Pledge](#)

[Stigma Free Me](#)

[Stigma Free Company](#)

[Stigma Free Store](#)

[Donate to NAMI](#)

Little Things Can Make A Big Difference

11 - One Idea of Possibility

I delight in telling the story of my niece to many people. It precedes the idea of "I think I can." It is the concept of I might be able to after all.

I am blessed to have a couple of delightful nieces, and they are like many of us in that they have had their challenges. My oldest niece is now a Nurse Practitioner with a Pediatric Specialty.

Earlier on in her life, her potential was not so clear to her as she graduated high school with very few career possibilities in mind. Like so many children her parents had divorced, and this left a shadow of confusion over the path for her life.

She was not thinking like the let's go to college crowd but more like the let's find a job and get to work thinkers. Then she talked about her future with my mother, and her concept of the future shifted.

She did not know nor did any of us in the family that my mother had been making steady deposits towards her education. I never knew the amount that was available nor is that important.

The information for my niece was tremendous as it launched a concept of possibility that shifted everything. Suddenly, my nieces' outlook on life was enhanced, and she thought that her life could be more and that her grandmother cared enough to help make that possible.

The idea that there was possibility grabbed hold of her mind and rekindled her dreams. She started to pursue optimistic ideas and succeeded.

The potential led to a higher blessing as her chosen career field nursing was understaffed, and there were incentive programs for possible students. The perfect plan she found was across the river in New Jersey, and the deal was that graduates would be offered a job within a certain number of years or their remaining tuition bill would be canceled.

When she graduated, the employment market had shifted, and there were too many nurses for the available jobs. They did not have a job for her, and they canceled her tuition balance.

She found a job elsewhere within a reasonable time, and her life became enhanced because of a single idea of possibility. Thank You, God!

I remain hopeful that subtle little shifts in operations can change the possibilities for prisoners just like my niece's whole life has been modified by a conversation with my mother, her grandmother.

12 - Prisoners Could Be Triaged

Triage is a French word that literally means sorting. It is frequently used in mass casualty situations to describe the sorting and priority assignment for the intensity of care needed.

Prisons can be compared somewhat to mass casualty situations as there are a lot of lives being impacted by the professional decisions that need to be made quickly and accurately. The sorting can determine the priority queue order for care.

Prisons can be so crowded that little events can trigger reactions that can have serious effects. Segmentation is offered as a barrier to help protect from or minimize consequences.

How does a practitioner know how to segment prisoners? A combination of tools might help in that regard to separate the most vulnerable in a progressive manner.

Segmentation and controlled circumstances alone might bring peace to some, and then diligent triage and further monitoring of events and conditions can help observers to quantify and evaluate reactions and possible causes or triggers.

In-depth Professional diagnosis and treatment may be less than immediately available in some cases, and that alone might allow some deterioration of conditions. It could help if there are standardized professionally designed, administered and supervised methods to help triage decisions.

Hopefully, these tools will enable the possibility of more care overall and more success in each effort.

13 - The Challenge Is To Make It Work

If all observers look at the progress that is made in seeking mental peace through the early steps of segmentation, then the success can be searched for the right next steps.

The challenge is to develop according to the needs of individual prisoners. What has not worked before, needs to be avoided now.

This is a program that will not need additional funding but could provide a return on time invested. The right matching of prisoners and opportunities will be essential if success is to be realized.

Prisoners who are allowed to provide purposeful opportunities can find peace in a natural way. Segmentation can be conducive to persistent service.

The combination potentials to benefit each individual facility are quite numerous and sophisticated effort will be helpful to maximize the benefits. Early participants in each prison may have much more opportunity than spectators.

Prisons are controlled by many different government agencies in the various locations, and there are a lot of historical precedents which has formed the rules of what presently exists. Early participants may have opportunities to create new criteria for the prisoners of the future.

We can explore possibilities by asking for ideas and discussing them in detail.

We will not succeed by doing everything the same old way and carrying the same old arguments forward that did not work before and will not work again. We need fresh perspectives and participants who can learn if they listen to the needs, wants and recommendation of residents.

Residual old thinking from opposing views does not offer any hope at all as standing opposition may be already entrenched and rigid.

Please seek to select fresh ideas that can be customized by stakeholders for a combined benefit view of new possibilities.

Concept development teams could choose goals that all will be able to accept. It is a good idea to avoid absoluteness and embrace performance standards.

Let others know that you have hope and understanding for all they share with you. Try to be both an investigator and a matchmaker of possibilities.

We can change the way the world sees mental health, and we can use segmentation to soften the slide of psychological deterioration.

Prisons present survival challenges for all prisoners, and the assembly of competitors in close proximity can trigger clashes. Those who have mental problems may have a negative impact that takes them further into crisis. Segmentation can increase options, limit deterioration and improve possibilities.

14 - Segmentation Could Influence A Lot

The ideas that I put forth may have little to offer the residents and staff members at your particular location as all facilities are different. I am hopeful that many prisoners will benefit from small changes that smooth their journey.

The stories and pictures of incarceration that are seen on the outside may be inaccurate, and it may be that some facilities have optimal support for all residents and staff members. I hope that where you live is fantastic.

It is normal for human beings to require a certain amount of private space which will vary with each person. Some people like being close together in situations.

Some things many might not necessarily understand is that mental illness is not the only issue for a lot of prisoners. A large number of prisoners have addiction issues along with their psychological and or emotional problems.

One frequently overlooked fact is that separating mental illness and addiction treatment could expedite treatment of both. Addiction issues can be somewhat addressed through treatment protocols that are generally accepted in society.

It could be a lot easier to get a Mental Health Practitioner or Medical professional to diagnose and prescribe addiction treatment than to get exhaustive Mental Treatment prescribed and initiated.

Now that is a start that could help the mentally ill and society.

15 - Declaration Of Program Start

It has been suggested to the administration that we could realign living arrangements to spread out the timing of how we use the limited space that we have and provide more quality uses for everybody.

The ideas presented are about using additional time blocks or shifts by realigning living patterns so there can be more private space for times that are agreed upon in advance.

There will still be a standard pattern for most prisoners. There will also be opportunities for prisoners to apply to be segmented for various size time blocks or projects.

There is no intention to make a universal change of any kind. The tentative plan is to move forward very slowly without any added expenses to the facility.

There can also be voluntary applications for program creation in time blocks that are not in conflict with the standard prison patterns.

The justification for this is that all will benefit when the human energy is spread out at times so there will be less density and therefore more receptivity to peaceful interactions.

Over time, minor adjustments will likely be adapted to accommodate areas that prove beneficial to the whole facility. We invite you to create ideas that we can consider. Acceptance will be contingent on the highest good for the whole community.

16 - Start-Up Questions For Prisoners

1. Would You like to participate in a living arrangement planning session?

2. Do you understand that there will be no new resources available for this project?

3. Are you willing to help develop this project?

4. Are you willing to submit ideas for consideration?

5. Do you understand that this will start without new funding and there are no guarantees?

6. Do You have a group you would like to assemble?

7. Do You Have a project you would like to plan and propose, and develop?

8. Will You Dialogue A 200 Word Concept Paper?

9. Are You Willing to Trade Rights For New Privileges?

10. Do You Fully Comprehend this will evolve very slowly unless prisoners provide positivity, purpose and optimal participation?

17 - Time Block Design

Time Blocks can be any size. All prisoners can be a candidate for participation. Proposals could be more likely to succeed if they contained a value for the community and not just the proposer. Helping others projects would be more likely to succeed. Program time blocks to start with:

> A. Two-hour program block of a new idea within the confines of the standard traditional prison time blocks.
>
> B. Three-hour program block of new design with a bag lunch within the confines of the standard traditional prison time blocks.
>
> C. Four-hour program block of new design with a bag lunch within the confines of the standard traditional prison time blocks.
>
> D. Five-hour program block of new design with a bag lunch within the confines of the standard traditional prison time blocks,
>
> E. Six-hour program block of unique design with a bag lunch within the confines of the regular conventional prison time blocks,
>
> F. Seven-hour program block of unique design with a bag lunch within the confines of the traditional prison time blocks,

18 - Opportunities Can Change A Lot

Your mind can filter things out or allow them into your life. Participants are invited to create choices for mental peace.

You are a powerful being even if you have been broken by your life circumstances or any of the events that occurred since your birth. The simple little powerful tool that can help you begin a new journey of personal discovery is mental peace.

Be kind first to yourself and soothe the pain that you know. Next look metaphorically for the burrs under your saddle that impact on the horse you ride.

As you treat yourself more kindly and spread the impact of your kindness to other beings on the planet, your personality will morph into a potential that you have not even dreamed possible. That new vision of possibility can take you into a feeling of vulnerability that is new and fresh and scary.

While that may sound exciting or ominous, the reality is that it may merely be an unknown quantity that you can assess, evaluate and develop into a future that you might like.

19 - Segmentation Could Change Surroundings

Even brain surgeons can find life boring when they are only doing the same things the same way in the same place every day just like the day before. Life is worth living when it is vibrant and fresh and dynamic and startlingly unpredictable.

Have you ever noticed that eating the same thing over and over again is boring? Even gourmet restaurants can be annoying when it is always the same repeatedly.

Life is vibrationally stimulated by new activities. When your sports team comes to your neighborhood and has tryouts for the kids, there becomes a new life of purpose that changes the vibrancy and joy of those who see it manifest.

Segmentation can allow diversity of many things to enhance the possibilities for the conceptualizing of a whole series of potentials that never before existed for any prisoners.

Segmentation can promote hope and potential and allow enough space for the manifestation of new life in the brains of old bodies. Further thoughts can breed new realities that can eventually manifest into new good for many.

20 - Segmentation Could Take Many Forms

The use of segmentation can evolve to a kind of respite from the prison norm that allows for a peaceful time out where one can separate from their usual associations and let their mind settle down and find some privacy, peace, and sanity.

Citizens in much less stressful situations need a break or mental health day. Prisoners also could benefit from reassessing the day to day grind.

I have some further ideas about the way segmentation can help, but for now, I would love to see what plans prisoners can develop that might catch fire and benefit the whole community

I would suggest to all that starting with a non-toxic mindset will be helpful to your success. Forgiveness of others can ratchet up your power to a new level of potential.

Segmentation can be a privilege that all disciplined residents could benefit from when they share ideas and peace and cooperation.

I would also enjoy seeing Dialogues of potentials for:
- One-night Segmentation
- Two-night Segmentation
- One-week Segmentations
- Writers Segmentations
- Efficiency Segmentations
- Enterprise Segmentations
- Family Segmentations
- Creativity Segmentations

21 - Thank You

For Considering These Ideas

22 - Don't Worry Ever

Ever

It Does Not Help Prayer Still Does!

Resource: http://www.Create-A-Prayer.com

23 - Resource Books

Distant Healing Sessions (or Join Mail List) – Write To mikewann@voicenet.com

Books by Rev. Mike at www.Amazon.com

Veterans Healing Six Pack
1. *Trauma Healing Options for VA Hospitals: Help for Veterans to Own Their Healing and their future.*
2. *Trauma Healing Action Steps for Veterans: Help to Start Healing*
3. *Trauma Healing Action Steps for Veterans: Empowerment*
4. *Trauma Healing Action Steps for Veterans: Forgiveness*
5. *Trauma Healing Action Steps for Veterans: Thought Freedom*
6. *Tea For Veterans: Welcome One Home*

PTSD Power Pack:
1. The PTSD Project: Turn Pain To Power
2. PTSD & Soul Retrieval: Putting One Back Together
3. PTSD & The Purple PAD: Calling all Scientists and PTSD Patients

Angel Raphael Speaks Volume 1: Take Courage! God Has Healing in Store for You!
Angel Raphael Speaks Volume 2: Take Courage! God Has Healing in Store for You!
Angel Raphael Speaks Volume 3: Take Courage! God Has Healing in Store for You!
Angel Raphael Speaks Volume 4: Angels, Addicts, Alcoholics & Prisoners – Oh Yeah!
Angel Raphael Speaks Volume 5: Prisoners Caring for Alcoholics - Australia In Miniature Projects Intro
Angel Raphael Speaks Volume 6: Prisoners Caring for Addicts - Australia In Miniature For Addicts
Reiki Journaling from Japan
Reiki Is Alive: God's Great Gift
Four Parts to Healing
Distant Healing: We Are All Connected
Stress Release Energy Work: How To Cope
Does Reiki Love Heal Cancer?
Group Consciousness
Salute To Philadelphia VA Medical Center: Thank You
Reiki Transcript for Reiki 2 & 3 Channels: Dr. Usui Is That You?
God Bless Kindle & Amazon
Puppies Are Different From People
If Your Dog Dies
Toy Guns Are Obsolete
Great Spirit Made Children With Red Skin: AND

The Cage of Fear: Is Not Locked
God Made Children Red, Yellow, Brown, Black & White: Greet Each Child With Kindness
Emergency Medical Kindness In The Cradle Of Liberty: Big City - Cracked Bell
Angels Are Always Around Addicts and Addicts: Help Is Near Now! Invite It In!
Angels Are Always Around Addicts and Alcoholics: Volume 2 - Tools To Help Re-Light Your Life
Prison Jobs Now: Providing Care For Addicts And Addicts
Controlled Care Communities Concept
Prison Possibilities Dialogue Series: Concept
Prison Possibilities Dialogue Series: Volume 2, 3, 4, 5 Dialogues
Prison Possibilities Voluntary Exile
Prison Possibilities Corrections Coaches
Prison Possibilities For Mexicans: Is A Boat Better Than A Wall?
Prison Possibilities Family Time: A Reason to Thrive!
Prison Genius Pool: "So Much Genius In Jail."
Prison Possibilities Access Control: Prisoner Access by Request
Prisoner's Lawyers Can Save The American Economy: Make A Buck Doing It & Be Thanked!
Prisoner Family Talks, Days, Stays & Vacations: Connecting Helps Healing
Prisoner Writing Projects: Write To Heal, Start Over & Reconnect
Prison Cell Clearing & Blessing: Clear Entities, Chase Ghosts, and & Create Sacred Space
Prisoner Professors: Show You Are Aware Create Change With Care
Prison Reiki? Maybe Someday? A Gateway To Help Heal Prisons & America?
Judges and An Angel Rule On Possibilities: We Can Cut Sentences & Prison Costs
Ideas For Prison Wardens: Leadership Is Not Easy
Solitary Community: Could Community Support Cut Costs and Issues?
Prison Project Communications Team: Communications Can Change Lives
Motivating & Empowering Prisoners? Invite Prisoners To Find Their Motivation
Prison Segmentation For Safety, And Sanity, Security, Peace, and Space
Prison Segmentation For Security
Dowsing for Prisoners; Answers from Above
Ex-Prisoner Possibilities With Real Estate Investors

Little Books at Kindle.com by Rev. Mike:
English Medical History Questionnaire For Non-English Speakers
English Language Helper For Non-English Speakers
Wise Wonderful Women Are The Well Of The Family
Answers for Test & Research: Dowsing Power
Crisis? Reiki! Baby? Reiki!
Bible References For Healing
Angel Raphael Speaks – Prisons
Angel Raphael Speaks – Veterans
The Saint Off Interstate 95

24 - Angels Please Prayers

Addict's

Angels of Healing Selected
Help Me to Stay Directed
Come To Me From The Sky
I Am Ready to Succeed Not Try
If I Don't Invite You In
I Might Not Win
I Have Been Lost For Too Long
Help Me To Stay Strong

Alcoholic's

Angels of Healing On High
Help Me to Stay Dry
Come To Me From The Sky
I Am Ready to Succeed Not Try
If I Don't Invite You In
I Might Not Win
I Have Been Lost For Too Long
Help Me To Stay Strong

From

http://AngelRaphaelSpeaks.com/AAAAAAA/

25 - Private Channeling

Angel Raphael Speaks a series of free messages that are channeled through Reverend Mike Wanner for the Highest good and Highest Healing of all concerned.

Many questions arise about Reverend Mike doing private channeling, and he does help with that so e-mail him.

Reverend Mike is available worldwide as a psychic channel, emotional release facilitator, spiritual energy practitioner & teacher, and public speaker. He looks forward to meeting you soon!

Email - mikewann@voicenet.com 215-342-1270 PRIVATE SPIRITUAL READINGS/channelings or Spiritual Healing Sessions: Telephone or in person. Rev. Mike is available for private, one-on-one intuitive sessions with you, his Guide Family, and your Guides. He helps by offering clarity on emotional situations about your life, your purpose, your spirituality, and the release of stuffed emotions and cellular memory.
Connect to the love of your Guides today!
Contact Rev. Mike for an appointment.

Sessions available:

Spiritual Readings
Angel Channeling
Distant Reiki Healing
Remote Clearing of Stuffed Emotions
Distant Clearing Cellular Memory
Distant Clearing Energy Blockages
Remote Clearing of the Chakras
Customized needs
Mastermind dowsing responses to yes/no direction finding questions.

Rev. Mike is a facilitator of healing. He brings you and the Divine together so that you can align with the Divine and have a great time and a great life. All healing is between you and God, as it should be. Go ahead and start without Rev. Mike. Visit his prayer site http://www.Create-A-Prayer.com. Take the first step NOW.

26 - Reverend Mike Wanner

Rev. Mike Wanner started his Metaphysical and Ministerial studies with Reiki in 1993 and had studied seven styles of Reiki in the U.S., Japan, Canada, Denmark and Australia. He is certified to teach. He became certified to teach Integrated Energy Therapy in 1999 and co-taught the first IET class of the new Millennium. Mike began dowsing in 2001.

Ordained as a Metaphysical Minister of the International Metaphysical Ministry and an Interfaith Minister of the Circle of Miracles Ministry, Rev. Mike practices and teaches spiritual energy therapies in the Philadelphia Area.

Rev. Mike holds ministerial degrees from the University of Metaphysics and the University of Sedona. He is a Pastoral Care Associate of Aria - Frankford Hospital. He taught at the National Academy of Massage Therapy and Health Sciences.

Rev. Mike was a faculty member of the Medical Mission Sister's Center for Human Integration's School of Integrated Body/Mind Therapies in Fox Chase, Philadelphia, PA for twelve years.

Rev. Mike is licensed by the teaching of Intuitional Metaphysics to practice Spiritual Healing and Scientific Prayer. Mike is also a Prayer therapist.

Rev. Mike was elected in 2007 to the status of "Fellow of the American Institute of Stress."

In 2008, Rev. Mike became a practitioner of Coincidental Recognition as he incorporated the CoRe System into his spiritual healing practice.

In 2009, Rev. Mike trademarked a new healing process called Quantum Quatro! Subtle Energy System Support®.

In 2011, Rev. Mike joined the outreach program known as the Health Advantage Group.

In 2012, Rev. Mike became a Certified Professional Coach by The Master Coaching Academy and Joined the Personal Empowerment Group.

Before his Metaphysical, Ministerial and Coaching studies, Rev. Mike worked for Sears Roebuck and Co. while in High School and after graduation, until he joined the U. S. Air Force in 1965. He returned to Sears from Vietnam in 1969 and stayed until 1978. His final Sears assignment was as an efficiency expert in Methods - Operational Research and Development.

He volunteered with Burholme Emergency Medical Services from 1969 and is still a Life Member and Board of Directors Member. He started a private ambulance company in 1975 and worked professionally in the field until 2001 when he devoted his full attention to real estate investing, healing, coaching, and writing.

May All Who Read This Be Blessed
AND SO IT IS!

www.ingramcontent.com/pod-product-compliance
Lightning Source LLC
Chambersburg PA
CBHW050034230526
45470CB00003B/1274